NELSON

British Columbia
In photographs

✧

Second Edition

✧

**Anne DeGrace &
Steve Thornton**

with

David R. Gluns

Copyright 2001 by Anne DeGrace and Steve Thornton
Photographs copyright individual photographers

All rights reserved. No part of this book may be reproduced or transmitted in any form by any means without permission in writing from the publisher, except by a reviewer, who may quote brief passages in a review.

Ward Creek Press
1124 McQuarrie Ave.
Nelson, B.C., Canada
V1L 1B2

National Library of Canada Cataloguing in Publication Data

DeGrace, Anne.
  Nelson British Columbia in photographs

  ISBN 0-9680739-2-1
  1. Nelson (B.C.)--Pictorial works. I. Thornton, Steve, 1950-
II. Gluns, David R. III. Title.
FC3849.N44D4 2001   971.1'62   C2001-910158-9
F1089.5.N35D4 2001
--

Cover photographs by David R. Gluns
Inside cover photograph by Steve Thornton
Photographs pages 3, 5, and 63 by David R. Gluns
Printed and bound in Canada by Friesens Printing

MESSAGE FROM THE PUBLISHERS

In this second edition, as in the first, we have tried to capture the heart of our community in sixty-four pages of colour photography.

Once again, picturing what makes Nelson special in only sixty-four pages has proved a singular challenge. We wanted to retain many of the first book's finest images, but to add exciting new pictures to the montage. We have tried to see our city with the fresh eyes of a visitor, while offering an insider's intimate point of view. And we've tried to celebrate Nelson's progress while honouring its history.

If we have succeeded at all, it is because we had great material to work with. This book is for Nelson, then, and for those who come to share a moment with us in a truly special place.

Anne DeGrace and Steve Thornton

Deep in the southeastern interior of British Columbia, in a shallow bowl formed by low, heavily wooded mountains and bisected by the western tip of a long, glacier-fed lake, is the city of Nelson, a garden of cultural and architectural treasures open to anyone who chooses to leave the beaten path.

Founded a century ago by a hard-working and adventurous crop of miners and loggers, the city has since turned to other pursuits, and through a gradual climb up the flank of a hill romantically called "Evening Ridge," Nelson has grown physically while expanding its horizons in the arenas of art, education, recreation, and business enterprise.

DAVID R. GLUNS

Geography imposes limits on Nelson's physical reach, however. The shore of Kootenay Lake marks a northern boundary, and to the south and east, the slopes of the Columbia Range form upper levels beyond which the efforts of civilization cannot easily proceed. These practical restraints have the secondary effect of limiting the population of Nelson, and in that regard, the city has shown remarkable stability, never straying far from an ideal number of about ten thousand.

The spirit of adventure that led to Nelson's birth is alive still, and the people who live and labour in this community try to keep a worldly view. Sister-city relationships with Shuzenji in Japan and Mutare in Zimbabwe announce that Nelson's door is open to the global community. An annual Artwalk festival puts the work of local artists at eye level for the strolling public every summer, and Streetfest reminds us that laughter is one of life's essential ingredients. The restoration of an old streetcar, which is now used as a lakeside tourist trolley, reflects an affection for tradition and history. And while industry quietly occupies the background, its practitioners take a back seat to no one, as indicated by their success in electronics, heavy equipment, and other fields.

Nelson's defining character, though, is not rooted in these qualities, for Nelson is, and always will be, what its physical shape makes it—a heritage city built upon a mountain slope. The character of Nelson is formed by its hundred-year-old architecture, the slabs of timber and granite and brick that, carved and fitted decades ago, have been covered up and then uncovered, rediscovered, and made into the centre-piece of a city that places a high value on its own story. And the character of Nelson is defined by the slopes of its streets: by the pedestrians who demonstrate an uncanny ability to stay upright on snowy sidewalks and an odd desire to walk up and down hills in all kinds of weather, by drivers who learn to negotiate fiendishly-steep routes with single-handed sangfroid, by kids who streak downhill on bicycles and skateboards as if the privileges of adulthood waited at the bottom, and by the measured pace of senior citizens who walk the sidewalks as if the hopefulness of childhood lay just around the next corner.

DAVID R. GLUNS

Finally, the character of Nelson is shaped by a collective esteem for the quality of life here, and a willingness to slow down and to view the past as more than simply where we have been. That is the essence of Nelson, the charm that brings people here and persuades them to look around with a fresh vision.

THE TOWN OF ALL TOWNS

COURTESY NELSON MUSEUM

Like many cities of the Canadian West, Nelson was founded on the promise of riches. Gold, found at nearby Forty-nine Creek in 1867, was an irresistible lure, and the next few years saw an unfolding drama of double dealings and even murder set against the backdrop of the Selkirk Mountains.

Gold petered out, but the discovery of silver on Toad Mountain brought prospectors back in greater numbers, and by the fall of 1887, the town known unofficially as Salisbury had taken shape in tents and rough cabins housing some three hundred miners.

According to the account of R.T. Lowery, an early newspaperman, "The camp was new and short of frills, boiled shirts, parsons, lawyers and prohibition orators. It had plenty of whisky, a few canary and other birds, and several pianos. All the rest of the population were mule skinners, packers, trail blazers, remittance men and producers, with a slight trace of tenderfeet. The police only slept in daytime."

Gilbert Malcolm Sproat, a gold commissioner and stipendiary magistrate, was sent out to establish a capital for the Kootenay Country in 1888. He settled on the town of Salisbury, but changed its name to Stanley, and in 1894 he reverentially described his hopes for the place in *The Miner*, a local newspaper: "My dream was

that here, where nature is so bountiful, there might be, could we but keep out newspapers and lawyers, the town of all towns for civilized habitation."

On Christmas Day, 1888, at the very fringe of the forest on Baker Street, Mary Jane Hanna served the community's first formal dinner. Guests included the area's only doctor.

Soon after that the town applied for a post office, and it was discovered that a Stanley already existed elsewhere in British Columbia. Another name was suddenly required, and so was borrowed from the lieutenant-governor, Hugh Nelson.

Although it took eleven days for a letter to get from Ainsworth to Nelson, a distance of some thirty-five miles, acquiring a post office was an early landmark that set the stage for progress. Nelson grew, and with it the industries of mining, logging and agriculture. Apples supplied another promise of gold for young immigrants, who saw markets in England for fruit from the Kootenays. Sternwheelers paddled up and down the lake, carrying produce and travellers. The area was thriving.

DAVID R. GLUNS

Civilization kept pace, and in 1897 *The Miner*, quoting a travelling piano tuner, reported that "there are more pianos in Nelson than there are in the homes, saloons, and concert halls in all the other towns in the district combined."

The first edition of *The Miner* rolled from the presses in June 1890. Seven years later it would report on the inauguration of its founder, John Houston, as Nelson's first mayor.

The dream of Gilbert Sproat—to "keep out newspapers and lawyers"—was impossible, of course. But today, many would agree that Nelson has indeed become "the town of all towns for civilized habitation."

DAVID R. GLUNS

DAVID R. GLUNS

DAVID R. GLUNS

Shades of green soothe the eye as one travels the eight-block length of Baker Street, where heritage is sculptured in the brick and mortar of hundred-year-old buildings. The Kirkpatrick-Wilson-Clements building (left, with Queen Anne-style tower and witch's cap) is a Nelson landmark, and attracted some important clients after opening in January 1901. The Canada Drug & Book Company occupied the entire first floor, while the second storey housed a number of physicians, lawyers, and "dental parlours," as well as the Prospector's Exchange. If one survived encounters there with stomach, appetite, teeth, and wallet intact, a dish of oysters could be enjoyed in the Palm Tea and Coffee Parlour. One is more likely to find a chocolate chip cookie than an oyster in a Baker Street "parlour" these days, but tasty food and timeless environments remain fashionable.

DAVID R. GLUNS

The presence of so many heritage buildings in Nelson has less to do with foresight and reverence for history than with economics. After the initial mining boom subsided and with it the excitement of newfound affluence, growth stabilized around 1920. As a result of a number of devastating fires, stone and brick replaced wood early in Nelson's building history, and this accounts for the presence of many historic buildings today.

As the century progressed, neither careful preservation nor rebuilding occurred, but rather a covering-up to cheaply modernize. Then, in the early 1980s Nelson was chosen as a pilot project for heritage revitalization. Metal sheeting and stucco were removed, revealing beautiful facades hidden for decades. Awnings and lamp standards were fashioned after historical items, lending an authentic look to the downtown area. It was Nelson's past that saw the city through its toughest economic times—and that carries it into the future.

Built around 1895, the Kootenay Exchange (right) is older than some of the antiques found there. A painstaking restoration earned this important building—the last example of Village Phase wood construction on Baker Street—a heritage award.

DAVID R. GLUNS

DAVID R. GLUNS

This Queen Anne-style front (right) is typical of commercial construction in 1897. The Baker Street second storey bay windows, once popular, are the last remaining in Nelson. Next door, echoing a pre-neon eon, fading historic signs still grace the brick walls of downtown buildings.

Cafés are islets of calm where locals and visitors can enjoy the aroma of fresh coffee and the companionable buzz of conversation. Outdoor seating has become popular—recalling, perhaps, an era when one might have enjoyed a glass of lemonade on a shady porch.

DAVID R. GLUNS

DAVID R. GLUNS

DAVID R. GLUNS

STEVE THORNTON

A handsome example of Late Victorian gothic architecture, St. Saviour's Anglican Church was built in 1898 and is located just a block away from the city's oldest Catholic Church, the Cathedral of Mary Immaculate (not shown).

Immortalized by the inept hosers of Steve Martin's 1987 film Roxanne, Nelson's firehall (facing page) was built in 1911 and has remained in continuous service ever since. The early crews of four horses, two wagons, and six men are long gone, but traces of their presence remain in the old building, and an antique firetruck museum preserves some early technology, including two 1944 Bickle Seagrave trucks.

The old brewery, built in 1899 just above the town's future firehall, is still in use, though its beer-making history is uneven. The Nelson Brewing and Ice Company was the first brewery in the interior with a refrigeration plant, which gave it a leg up on competition in the ice market. In the 1950s the brewery closed, but nearly forty years later, it was brought back into operation (see pg 28).

JEREMY ADDINGTON

DAVID R. GLUNS

INSET COURTESY CAPITOL THEATRE

Plush red seats, gilt–framed murals, chandeliers, and a ceiling painted with clouds met Capitol Theatre patrons in 1927. Through the years, the advent of talkies, and the Depression, the theatre provided entertainment in films and in performances by such companies as Nelson Little Theatre and the Rossland Light Opera. After the Civic Theatre scooped the Famous Players contract in the Forties, the smaller but more ornate Capitol fell silent.

In 1980, amid the bloom of heritage revitalization, the city bought the building and a group of volunteers formed the Capitol Theatre Restoration Society. Today, the Capitol boasts fine acoustic technology and an interior lovingly restored to its original design. Touring performances, local music and amateur theatre, art exhibitions, forums, and political debates ensure that it's seldom quiet.

Bitter squabbles broke out between architect and foreman on the construction site of what would one day be Nelson's City Hall. Eventually charged with using strong language, the foreman was convicted and fined $10 in magistrate's court.

In 1902, the beautiful Romanesque-style building opened as a Post Office. Sixty years later, it became Nelson's City Hall, continuing an established tradition of lively debate.

While inheriting the quaint charm of bygone years, today's City Hall bustles with the activities of mayor, clerk, treasurer, and parking meter cops. It is open to the public, and one is as likely to see locals attending—and perhaps debating—a council meeting as standing at a clerk's wicket, paying—and perhaps debating—an electrical bill.

DAVID R. GLUNS

JEREMY ADDINGTON

Impressive and beautiful in detail, the Bank of Montreal at Baker and Kootenay streets suggests nothing of its humble beginnings. Yet it must have seemed an expedition to the heart of nowhere for A.H. Buchanan, an accountant with the bank in Vancouver, when he set out to take up his new position at Nelson. With roads blocked by heavy snow, the intrepid Buchanan strapped on snowshoes and trekked eighty kilometres (fifty miles) from Northport, Washington, to establish the Nelson branch in 1892.

His arrival may have been impressive, but his assets were modest: $11.50 in cash. Undeterred, "Buck" Buchanan borrowed a further $2.50, installed a safe in the local barber shop, and opened for business. His first customers were packhorse drivers, who deposited their earnings with him.

In 1899, acclaimed architect Francis Rattenbury, noted for such edifices as the B.C. Parliament Buildings and the Empress Hotel in Victoria, designed the bank building that stands today, as well as the Nelson Courthouse (facing page), completed in 1902. Adding to the dignified appearance of the Courthouse is a cloak of creeping ivy, set alight by autumn frost.

JEREMY ADDINGTON

DAVID R. GLUNS

From fire in the sky to fire in the street, spectacle and celebration enthrall the residents of a community where a hundred years can slip away in the wink of an eye. Streetfest brings international street performers to Nelson for a few days each July, and during Heritage Days, clothing styles popular when the town was young are briefly reborn. On some weekends, the social calendar becomes so full that it's impossible to see everything—a happy dilemma.

DAVID R. GLUNS

DAVID R. GLUNS

STEVE THORNTON

Hotrod builder Andy Popoff has turned his garage into an artful billboard of automotive memories—and a part-time customizing shop where he tackles projects like this 1940 Ford.

DAVID R. GLUNS

STEVE THORNTON

Nelson's reputation as an arts community is rooted in its long-time resident artists, who provide a cultural backbone. Summertime Artwalk exhibitions have proved to businesses that art on the walls can bring customers into shops. Many now display artworks all year long.

Locally crafted items are sold in stores, and a twenty year old craft cooperative attests to the staying—and earning—power of creative enterprise.

STEVE THORNTON

Nelson Brewing Company's Tim Pollock keeps the lid on kegs of draught beer waiting for shipment to pubs across B.C., where high demand ensures it won't sit for long. The company opened in 1991 on the premises of the original Nelson Brewing Company, which brewed such popular brands as Porter XXX from the 1890s to 1955. A small operation, today's NBC enjoys success due to the quality of its refreshment.

Art education has been close to the community heart of Nelson for decades. Kootenay School of the Arts, situated in the old city jail, attempts to prove that while crime doesn't pay, art might, through programs intended to produce professional working artists in fine arts, writing, craft, and design.

Educational opportunities in the arts also include Selkirk College's professional music school, the Capitol Theatre's summer youth program, and dance classes in everything from tap to belly. Students may strut their stuff with some improv theatre, a little curbside fiddling, or a hot jazz night at a local café.

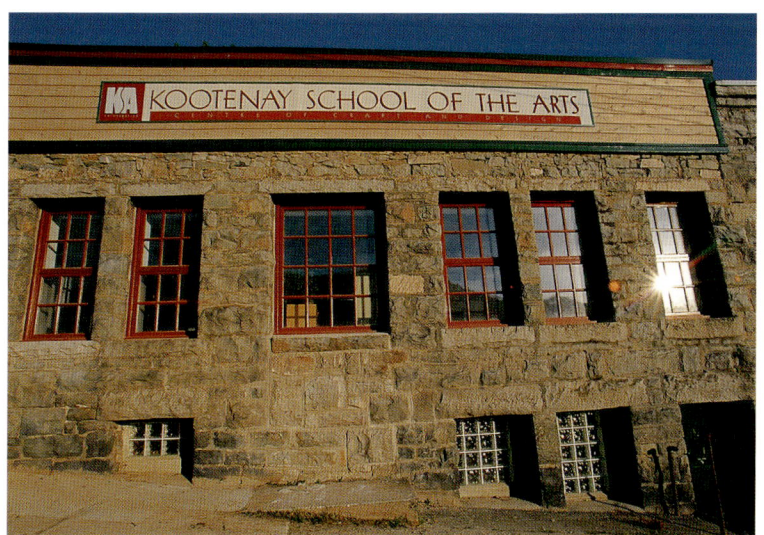

DAVID R. GLUNS

DAVID R. GLUNS

GILLIAN BROWNING

In May 1900, houses on hilly Victoria Street (left) rented for twenty-five dollars a month and were quaintly described in the Nelson *Tribune*: "new five-room cottage, hot and cold water, bathroom and sewer connection."

Just north of Nelson, Selwyn Blaylock built the home he called Lakewood (below) in 1934. A blend of Tudor and Craftsman architecture, the mansion, surrounded by elegant gardens, is a North Shore landmark.

At right, nature decorates a heritage home setting with fall leaves, a perennial playground for generations of children.

DAVID R. GLUNS

DAVID R. GLUNS

DAVID R. GLUNS

Throwing light back into the night, Nelson glitters after sunset. While starry skies are blinded by the candlepower of larger cities, the celestial spectacle remains undiminished in the scarcely-populated Kootenays—though earthly lights can occasionally dazzle. When reflected off the dark waters of Kootenay Lake, even common streetlights become beautiful.

DAVID R. GLUNS

JEREMY ADDINGTON

Heritage houses are valued by Nelson residents, considered as much a part of the city's identity as its revitalized downtown. These grand old homes are featured in a heritage tour for visitors. Bank manager "Buck" Buchanan was the first resident of this Late Victorian–style house, owned by the Bank of Montreal and named "Hochelaga" after the Mohawk village that eventually became Montreal. The imposing structure was well suited for the important social events that were a bank manager's obligation, and perhaps pleasure, to host.

JEREMY ADDINGTON

Built in 1891 by prominent businessman J. Fred Hume, this Hoover Street house, the first in Nelson with hot and cold running water, was a wedding present for his new wife Lydia. Hume later sold the house to Charles Ink, a printer, who with John Houston and W.G. Allen started Nelson's first newspaper, *The Miner*. What was once a wonder of modern construction now holds the distinction of being Nelson's oldest heritage home.

DAVID R. GLUNS

This High Victorian–style house was built in 1898 for John Houston, the city's first mayor. Houston served four terms as mayor, ran two newspapers, and championed the rights of ordinary people, becoming Nelson's most famous citizen. Built on a corner lot, the house was intended to be viewed from two directions, so its gabled corner was designed as a centrepiece. Though some of the original craftsmanship has been tempered by time, the character prevails as it stands at the corner of a new century.

Nelson's mild, snowy winters are generally taken in stride, but shovels are kept handy for snow removal—or use as a leaning post while chatting with a neighbour.

STEVE THORNTON

DAVID R. GLUNS

From old-fashioned garden produce to New Age crystals, the offbeat and the ordinary are for sale at the Tree Of Life farmer's market on Saturday mornings. The outdoor market occupies a park-like setting next to roaring Cottonwood Falls.

DAVID R. GLUNS

DAVID R. GLUNS

Lakeside and Gyro Park gardens are year-round projects in which full-time gardeners take artistic pride. Gyro Park paths meander through pockets of pansies and ornamental shrubs in the shade of birch and pine trees, while Lakeside Park presents an open blaze of colour and an eclectic mix of English Oak, Norway Maple, Black Walnut, Chinese Chestnut, London Plane and Ginko amidst indigenous varieties. Neighbourhood yards are alight with patches of red and yellow all summer long.

DAVID R. GLUNS

A vision of history preserved resulted in the restoration and lakeside route of Streetcar No. 23, whose last Baker Street run took place in 1949. Before its painstaking restoration, No. 23 was in service as a chicken coop on Nelson's North Shore.

DAVID R. GLUNS

More than a thousand individuals and a dozen community groups joined hands to create Nelson's scenic Waterfront Pathway, a stroller's dream of quiet coves and pleasant viewpoints. Nearby playing fields may be filled with soccer, baseball or rugby players, while pathside stone plaques offer glimpses into shoreline sights of a century ago.

DAVID R. GLUNS

DAVID R. GLUNS

Ahhh ... summer in Nelson. Sunny days and cool mountain nights create an enviable climate in which to enjoy the warm sand of Lakeside beach or the chilly waters of Kootenay Lake, which rise to a shivery 18 degrees by August. Some say it's better water to be on than in, and the lake's wide bays and wave-swept reaches are a freshwater boater's delight.

DAVID R. GLUNS

DAVID R. GLUNS

DAVID R. GLUNS

Fingertips straining for a crevice, a climber scales granite cliffs while Nelson basks in evening light far below.

DAVID R. GLUNS

Line drifting lazily behind him, an early–morning boater enjoys calm water on Kootenay Lake near Nelson's most visible and best-known landmark.

The 630-metre bridge was eagerly awaited, and opinions about its construction flowed as freely as the unimpeded Kootenay River, but less reliably. Lieutenant-Colonel Fred Lister, for example, suggested a pontoon bridge in 1931.

When it finally came, at a cost of $4 million, there were no pontoons—nor, as some had suggested, was wood the material of choice. What was opened on November 7, 1957, was a steel span, elevated five hundred fifty metres (1,805 feet) above sea level—or just over eighteen metres (60 feet) above the local high-water mark.

For a few years, drivers paid a fifty cent toll for the privilege of using the orange bridge. Just before twelve midnight on March 31, 1963, a few locals, including George Coletti, rolled up to the gate and handed toll–taker Clarence Ward the final tickets. At one minute past midnight on April Fool's Day, a green light was switched on, RCMP Constable John Jack drove through without stopping, and forever after no one has been legally charged for crossing Kootenay Lake.

DAVID R. GLUNS

Mountainous terrain is ideal for trek by horse, foot, or bicycle, and clean lakes and rivers offer a refreshing break after an uphill climb. In backcountry seclusion, clothing is optional. Glorious lupines (facing page) colour the hillsides in late spring.

DAVID R. GLUNS

Located just north of Nelson, Kokanee Glacier Provincial Park is a vastly rewarding environment for outdoors enthusiasts who venture there—but also a demanding one that has taken lives. At right, Kokanee Glacier is an icon of wilderness grandeur.

A snowshoer (left) pauses in a landscape of harsh and sublime beauty. Around Nelson, opportunities abound for winter recreation. Whitewater ski hill, south of town, offers exceptional back country access, and more than forty runs through powder snow.

DAVID R. GLUNS

Eyes on the ball, a golfer at Granite Pointe golf course seems unaware of the magnificence behind him. Below, the Osprey 2000 crosses Kootenay Lake, ferrying people and vehicles from Kootenay Bay to Balfour. At right, an osprey's-eye view of Nelson.

DAVID R. GLUNS

DAVID R. GLUNS

53

DAVID R. GLUNS

Each fall, thousands of bright red Kokanee salmon journey up Kootenay creeks to spawn. Hundreds of people watch the spectacle each year at Kokanee Creek Park, where interpretive tours draw visitors to the spawning channel. After an arduous trip, these beautiful fish die, leaving behind their eggs which in turn will silver the creeks with millions of fry in the spring.

Ospreys are a common yet always impressive sight on Kootenay Lake. Returning in the spring from South American wintering grounds, the fish hawk may find a Canada goose in its old nest atop a lakeshore piling—a situation that can lead to a noisy confrontation and eviction of the goose. At the Kootenay Bay ferry terminal, nesting ospreys provide a boat's-eye view for passengers, and their behaviour, from courtship rituals to flying lessons for the young, is easy to observe. With a two-metre (six-foot) wingspan, the osprey is a spectacular sight when hunting Kokanee.

DAVID R. GLUNS

DAVID R. GLUNS

56

DAVID R. GLUNS

DAVID R. GLUNS

At a patio table, friends enjoy dinner and companionship while the evening air cools over Nelson. Mountain peaks catch the last of the sunlight, and then, as darkness falls, the air and the water become still.

STEVE THORNTON

DAVID R. GLUNS

In the poem My Symphony, William Henry Channing (1810 - 1884) expressed a philosophy that has been considered by some to define life lived in Nelson, this town of all towns.

My Symphony

To live content with small means;
to seek elegance rather than luxury,
and refinement rather than fashion;
to be worthy, not respectable, and
wealthy, not rich; to study hard,
to think quietly, talk gently, act frankly;
to listen to stars and birds, to babes and
sages, with open heart; to bear all cheerfully,
do all bravely, await occasions, hurry never.
In a word, to let the spiritual,
unbidden and unconscious, grow up
through the common.
This is to be my symphony.

DAVID R. GLUNS

DAVID R. GLUNS

CONTRIBUTING PHOTOGRAPHERS

Jeremy Addington
Gillian Browning
David R. Gluns
Steve Thornton

ACKNOWLEDGEMENTS

Much of this edition is new, but much has not been changed, and so our gratitude to those who contributed to the original book should be restated: Thanks to Shawn Lamb, Doug Jones, Fiona Richards, Angela Lockerbie, Margaret Chrumka, and George and Kay Coletti. Thanks also to Robert Inwood, Tim Kendrick, Don Tonsaker, and others who answered questions and offered good wishes for this second edition. And finally, we wish to express our ongoing appreciation for the community of Nelson.